Ice-Cream Cones for Sale!

Ice-Cream Cones For Sale!

ELAINE GREENSTEIN

ARTHUR A. LEVINE BOOKS

An Imprint of Scholastic Press

· Library of Congress Cataloging-in-Publication Data · Greenstein, Elaine. Ice cream cones for sale!/by Elaine Greenstein.—1st ed. p. cm. Summary: Reveals who really invented the ice cream cone, even before the 1904 St. Louis World's Fair where five people claim they did so. ISBN 0-439-32728-8 1. Ice cream cones–History–Juvenile literature. [1. Ice cream cones–History.] I. Title. · TX795.G86 2003 · 637'.4–dc21 · 2002012556 · 3 5 7 9 10 8 6 4 2 04 05 06 07 · Printed in Singapore 46 · First edition, June 2003 · The text type is set in 17-point Golden Cockerel. The illustrations are monoprints overpainted with gouache. The photograph accompanying the author's note is from the Montegue Lyon collection, Missouri Historical Society, St. Louis. Book design by Kristina Albertson

St. Louis World's Fair

To Érico

Have you heard about the great ice-cream cone controversy? It all began on April 30, 1904, opening day of the world's fair in St. Louis, Missouri. There were more than fifty ice-cream sellers at the fair and, they say, a lot of waffle-makers. At some point the two came together to form an ice-cream cone.

But who came up with the idea first?

ARNOLD FORNACHOU   ERNEST HAMWI   CHARLES MENCHES   ABE DOUMAR   DAVID AVAYOU
                                    & LADY FRIEND

Some folks say it was a young man named Arnold Fornachou.
Arnold said that he ran out of dishes at his ice-cream stand
one warm day. So he asked Ernest Hamwi at the next stand
over to make waffles for him, which he rolled into cones.

But Ernest Hamwi, a waffle-maker from Syria, said it was his idea. He took one of his warm waffle cookies, which he called zalabia, rolled it up, and offered it to his neighbor. "Arnold, my boy, see if your scoop fits in this."

After that, no one wanted a dish, everyone wanted a cone.

So they say . . .

But other people claim Abe Doumar dreamed up the cone. Abe sold souvenirs at the fair during the day. At night he hung around talking to the waffle-makers and watching the hootchy-cootchy dancers.

Supposedly, one night Abe got the great idea, which he shared with Ernest Hamwi, who liked the idea so much he gave Abe one of his waffle irons to take home to New Jersey.

So they say . . .

But there were still more competing claims! David Avayou came all the way from Turkey to St. Louis. On the way, he stopped in France. He said he got the idea from all those fancy paper cones he saw used in Paris.

Ooh-la-la . . .

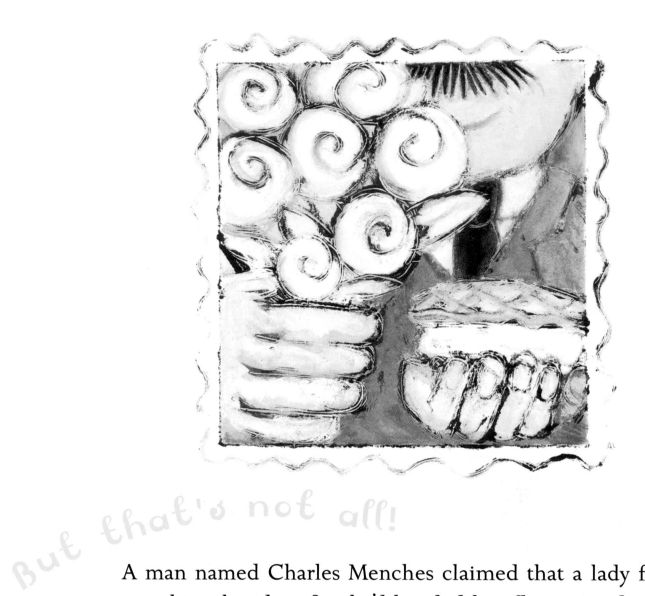

But that's not all!

A man named Charles Menches claimed that a lady friend gave him the idea after he'd handed her flowers and an ice-cream sandwich at the same time. She took off the top of the sandwich and rolled it into a vase for the flowers and rolled the bottom into a cone for the ice cream.

Arnold, Ernest, Abe, David, and Charles and his lady friend were all at the fair.

But who is the true inventor?

None of them! The honor belongs to a man named Italo Marchiony.

In 1895, Italo came to the United States with a suitcase and his grandmother's recipe for ice cream. Soon he had his own pushcart in New York City.

"Ice cream! Four cents a dish! Get your ice-cold ice cream!"

Every day, from Wall Street to Houston Street, Italo scooped ice cream, and then he waited. And waited and waited. He waited for his customers to finish their treat and return the dish before he could push his cart ahead and sell more ice cream.

The truth is that I couldn't find letters or articles about how Italo actually came up with his big idea, but this is what i imagine. . . .

Every afternoon, Italo stops at Louie's Bake Shop.

Perhaps Italo gives Louie a dish of ice cream,

and Louie gives Italo a cookie.

Maybe Italo uses Louie's sink.

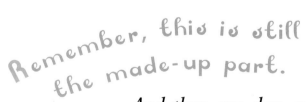

Remember, this is still the made-up part.

And then one day, a big, black dog bumps into Italo, the dish slips from Italo's hand, the scoop flies in the air. Somehow Italo catches the dish. Louie catches the ice cream on the cookie.

Italo can't get the idea out of his mind. Maybe Louie shows Italo that you can shape a cookie when it's warm and that some cookies will bend more than others. Louie starts making cookies for Italo so he can try the idea.

Imagine — no dishes! no waiting! no washing!

I imagine that Italo sells so many cones that Louie can't make the cookies fast enough. So, Italo invents a special mold for Louie to make ten cookies at once.

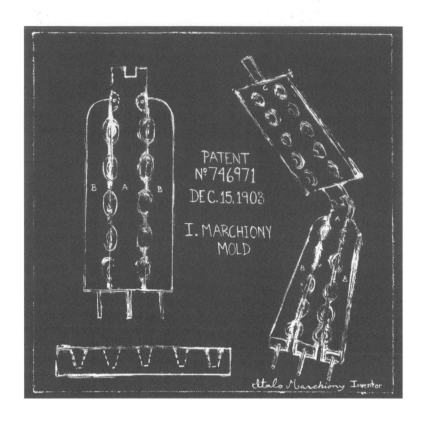

This last part is true. . . .

The mold was great! In September 1903, Italo sent a copy of the design to the U. S. Patent Office so he could stake his claim as the inventor of the ice-cream cone. Documents prove Italo was awarded the patent on December 15, 1903 — months before the world's fair opened in St. Louis.

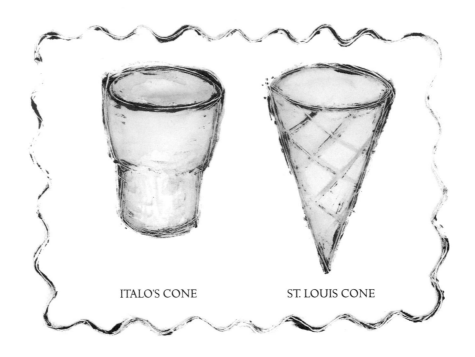

ITALO'S CONE   ST. LOUIS CONE

Of course, as you know now, that didn't stop all those other people in St. Louis from claiming it was their invention. Probably, as far as they knew, they were first.

And, to add one more tasty wrinkle to our story: If you look closely, it seems we could be talking about two different kinds of cones. Italo's is more like the kind we now call a "wafer" cone. And the St. Louis version is more like what we call a "sugar cone" or . . . you guessed it—a waffle cone!

1.

2.

Lick around the bottom edge of the scoop to prevent drips.

Don't lick too hard, the ice cream will fall out.

everyone agrees on this advice:

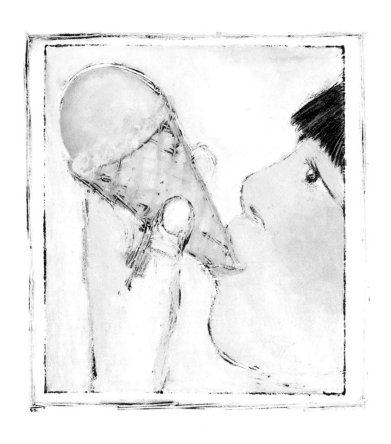

3.

4.

Never bite the bottom of the cone while there's ice cream in it.

And there's no better treat than an ice-cold ice-cream cone.

Yummm!

Author's Note

Thank you to Joseph Marchiony, the Hoboken Historical Museum, and the Missouri Historical Society for their help with my research. I found many articles and stories about the invention of the ice-cream cone. Some seemed solidly based in fact; others could not be proven. I used the stories for which I could find a second source that supported the claims.

I wish I could have included a story told to me by Joseph Marchiony, Italo's nephew, who heard it from Italo's daughter Jane. The story goes that Italo himself had an ice cream stand at the St. Louis Fair in 1904, but when he ran out of his patented pressed cones, he asked a waffle maker to supply him with rolled waffles. Unfortunately, I could not find records confirming that Italo was at the 1904 Fair. Likewise, there is a Hamwi family story that Ernest Hamwi came to the fair in order to create mosaics for a display and that it was his son who came up with the waffle idea. There is no confirming record of this either. In fact, while the Missouri Historical Society's records show many vendors selling ice cream at the St. Louis World's Fair, no one is officially listed as selling ice-cream cones. There is, however, the anonymous photograph shown below — so we know that cones were there!

The folks I've written about made their claims and told their stories in books, magazines, and newspapers published long after the 1904 world's fair:

Birk, Dorothy Daniels. *The World Came to St. Louis: A Visit to the 1904 World's Fair.* St. Louis: Bethany Press, 1979.

Dickson, Paul. *The Great American Ice Cream Book.* New York: Atheneum, 1972.

French, Janet Beighle. "Double Dip of Cone History." *Cleveland Plain Dealer,* 18 July 1993, Sunday edition, sec. G, p. 1.

Funderburg, Anne Cooper. *Chocolate, Strawberry, and Vanilla: A History of American Ice Cream.* Bowling Green, Ohio: Bowling Green State University Popular Press, 1995.

Gustaitis, Joseph. "Who Invented the Ice Cream Cone?" *American History Illustrated,* Summer 1988, 42-44.

"Italo Marchiony, 86, Made Ice Cream Cone." *New York Times,* 29 July 1954, p. 23.

Marchiony, Italo. "Mold." U. S. Patent 746,971. 15 December 1903.

Misc-File. *St. Louis Commerce,* September 1981, 16.

Misc-File. *St. Louis Commerce,* October 1981, 18.

Paretti, Jane Marchiony. "The Man Who Invented the Ice-Cream Cone." *Hoboken History* 2, no. 2 (Winter 1992): 3.

Quinzio, Jeri. "The Ice Cream Cone Conundrum." *Radcliffe Culinary Times* 10, no. 1 (Spring 2000): 6.

Scales, Pat. "Ice Cream Cones Hold Oh-So-Sweet Success." *Washington Post,* 9 July 1985, late edition, sec. D, p. 7.

Snow, Richard F. "King Cone." *Invention and Technology,* Fall 1993, 5.

Terry, Dickson. "How Old Are Ice Cream Cones?" *St. Louis Post-Dispatch,* 15 March 1954: Sunday edition, sec. H, p. 3.

Thompson, Bryce. "The Great Ice Cream Cone Controversy." *The Sundae School Newsletter–National Ice Cream and Yogurt Retailers Association Monthly Bulletin* 15, no. 3 (March 1994): 2.

Tice, Patricia M. *Ice Cream for All.* Rochester, N.Y.: The Strong Museum, 1990.

United Press International. "The Ice Cream Cone: Who Invented It?" *St. Louis Post-Dispatch,* 12 December 1977, final edition, sec. D, p. 3.

United Press International. "St. Louis's Claim as Birthplace of the Ice Cream Cone Is Challenged." *St. Louis Post-Dispatch,* 30 July 1954, final edition, sec. A, p. 1.

Viets, Elaine. "Melting Claims on First Ice Cream Cone," *St. Louis Post-Dispatch,* 4 June 1978, final edition, p. 30.

Two Homes

First edition 2001

Library of Congress Cataloging-in-Publication Data
Masurel, Claire.
Two homes / Claire Masurel ; illustrated by Kady MacDonald Denton. —1st ed.
p. cm.
Summary: A young boy named Alex enjoys the homes
of both of his parents who live apart but love Alex very much.
ISBN 0-7636-0511-5
[1. Divorce—Fiction. 2. Parent and child—Fiction. 3. Dwellings—Fiction.]
I. Denton, Kady MacDonald, ill. II. Title.
PZ7.M4239584 Tw 2001
[E]—dc21 00-041398

2 4 6 8 10 9 7 5 3 1

Printed in Belgium

This book was typeset in Godlike.
The illustrations were done in ink, watercolor, and gouache.

Candlewick Press
2067 Massachusetts Avenue
Cambridge, Massachusetts 02140

Two Homes

Claire Masurel   illustrated by Kady MacDonald Denton

CANDLEWICK PRESS
CAMBRIDGE, MASSACHUSETTS

Here I am! I am Alex.

This is Daddy.

And this is Mommy.

Daddy lives here.
Sometimes I'm with Daddy.

Mommy lives there.
Sometimes I'm with Mommy.

So . . . I have *two homes!*

I have *two* front doors.

My coat goes here.

My coat goes there.

I have *two* rooms.

My room at Daddy's.

My room at Mommy's.

I have *two* favorite chairs.

A rocking chair at Daddy's.

A soft chair at Mommy's.

I have lots of friends.

Friends come and play at Daddy's.

Friends come and play at Mommy's.

I have *two* kitchens.

Daddy and I cook here.

Mommy and I cook there.

I have *two* bathrooms.

I have a toothbrush at Daddy's.

I have a toothbrush at Mommy's.

And I have *two* telephone numbers.

Mommy calls me at Daddy's house.

Daddy calls me at Mommy's house.

I love Daddy.

And I love Mommy.
No matter where I am.

We love you, Alex.

We love you wherever we are.

And we love you wherever you are.

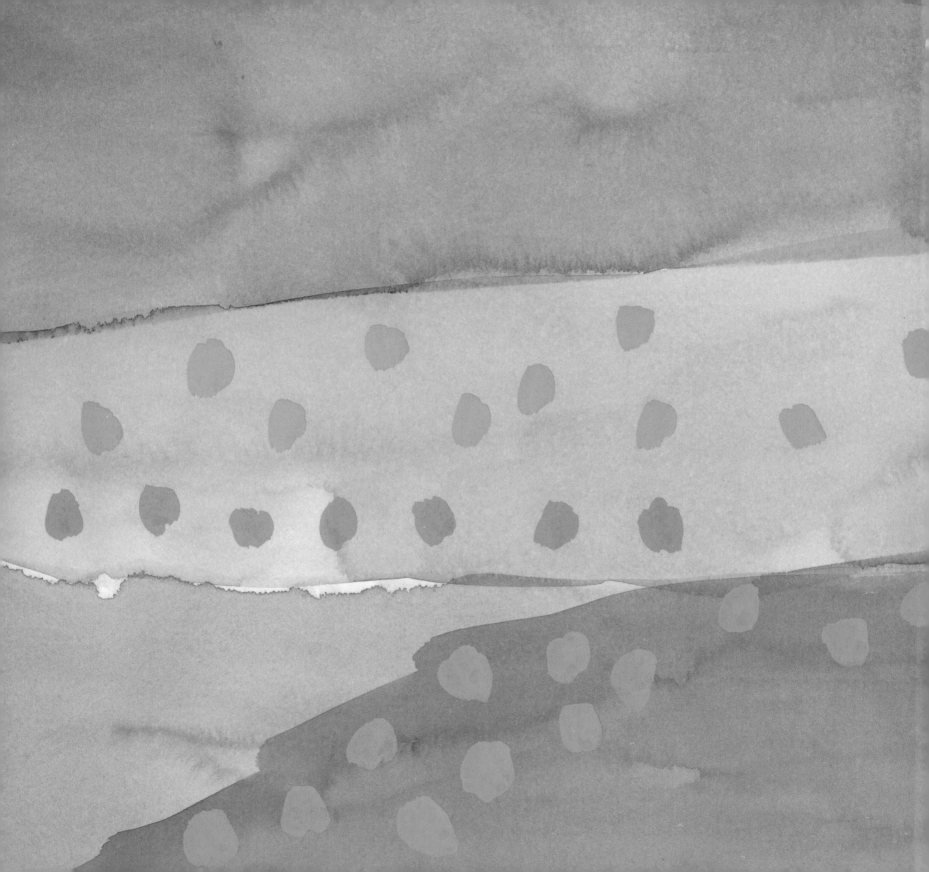